FROM THE
THEATER OF MY MIND

Starring
Frank Lloyd Kramer
Poet

Co-Starring
Vickie Leigh Krudwig
Illustrator

From the Theater of My Mind
Text copyright © 2002 by Frank Lloyd Kramer
Art copyright © 2002 by Vickie Leigh Krudwig

Library of Congress   2002114190
ISBN   0-9644903-1-5

Design by
Vickie Leigh Krudwig and Lynn Sauve

Contributing Editors
Jessica L. Krudwig
Lynn Sauve
Ruth Vail

Printed in the USA

Castle Publishing Company
Denver, Co 80220
(303) 394-1187
cajunpoet@aol.com

Sweet Success Press, Inc.
Denver, Co 80260
1 (303) 469-2223
1 (800) 505-5044

DEDICATION

For Lynn, Liz, Mom and Vickie
My earliest and loudest fans.

 And to the Muse,
Wherever you are.
FLK

For Lynn, Frank, and my family,
My constant source of inspiration.

A special thanks to the Lantzy's for their
support and willingness to chauffer my
children while I worked on this project!
VLK

3

FRANKIE POEMS

Funny poems
And sunny poems
That make you laugh a while

Caring poems
And sharing poems
That give your heart a smile.

TABLE OF CONTENTS

SCENE ONE: GOTTA GIGGLE

SCENE TWO: SCHOOL AID

SCENE THREE: TUMMY TEASERS

SCENE FOUR: ANIMALS, BIRDS AND BUGS

SCENE FIVE: PLAYING OUTSIDE

SCENE SIX: PONDERING

ABOUT THE AUTHOR AND ILLUSTRATOR

SCENE ONE: GOTTA GIGGLE

Gotta giggle
Tummy wiggle
Laugh from 8 to 5
Gotta giggle
Tummy wiggle
Glad to be alive

THE LAUGHING KID

Have you ever heard the story
   Of the funny little kid
Who couldn't even say his name
   'Cause laugh is all he did?

He laughed whenever he was sick
   And laughed when he was sad,
He laughed when he was feeling well
   And laughed when he was mad.

He came with me to church one day
   I tried to keep him quiet,
He laughed at what the preacher said
   He thought it was a riot.

He laughed so much at dinnertime
   He almost split his britches,
His family couldn't eat their food
   'Cause they were all in stitches.

He went to see a picture show
   Where all the people cried,
He couldn't stop his laughing though
   He tried and tried and tried.

He accidentally walked into
   A solid wall of stone,
He said it made him laugh because
   He hit his funny bone.

The doctors all examined him
   And finally gave up hope,
He laughed aloud at what they said -
   He thought it was a joke.

He laughed at all the teachers,
   'Twas more than they could take,
He giggled at the principal -
   It was a big mistake.

They finally kicked him out of school
Because he was outrageous,
They didn't want to take the chance
That he would be contagious!

HAIR

My uncle's hair is everywhere
Except where it should go.
There is no hair upon his head
It doesn't want to grow.

It grows around his ears so that
He's looking like a mutt.
It's growing on his nose and toes
And growing on his butt.

He doesn't have a moustache
Or a tiny bit of beard.
The only places hair will grow
Are absolutely weird.

No one knows a barber that
Will cut my uncle's hair,
And all the barbers said to him,
"I will not cut it there!"

BODY SHOP

My uncle had a knee replaced
   The old one kind of failed,
He also needs a newer hip
   He's waiting for a sale.

I think that I will visit him
   And ask him where to go
To buy some bigger parts for me-
   Mine are growing slow.

I'll check up on that body shop
   That's right across the street
Maybe I can get a deal
   On bigger hands and feet!

ALL MIXED UP

I'm going to do my hamburger
   And have some homework helper.
When daddy comes to fix the car
   I think I'll go and help her.

If you need a ride somewhere,
   I can drive you crazy.
I've got to turn my burger in
   At school to Mr. Daisy.

I'm going to go to sleep right now
   And write this crazy rhyme,
But if it's got you all mixed up
   Just read it one more time!

NEGOTIATION

My father likes his music
My mother likes her quiet.

My mother told my father:

*"Turn that music down right now
Or you'll be on a diet!"*

A-A-A-A-CHOOO!

I sneezed my nose
Right off my face,
It's somewhere on the
Floor!
I hope that I can
Find my nose
Before I sneeze some
More!

RIGHT WAY

Two wrongs
Don't make a right
They say-

But

Three left turns
Will get you headed
That way.

THE WATER CYCLE

I went to get a glass of water
   From the kitchen sink,
As I drank the water down
   Then I began to think,

I wonder where this water was
   Before it came to me.
What ocean, lake, stream or pond
   What bay or gulf or sea?

Before it turned to vapor and
   Became a cloud up there,
This water could have been around
   To wash my underwear!

HALLOWEEN

Twenty screaming children have
    Been knocking at my door-
Bags are full of candy and they're
    Looking for some more.

"Hello children, how are you,
    Happy Halloween,
I have a bowl of broccoli and
    A cup of collard greens.

Help me eat this liver, I would
    Love for you to stay."
Twenty screaming children then
    Began to run away.

OLDER BROTHER

My older brother used to be
Twice as old as me.
When he became six years old
I was only three.

Now I'm eight and he's eleven -
Less than twice as old,
When I am nine, he is twelve;
Less percent I'm told.

No longer does he treat me like
A bratty younger brother.
He thinks someday we'll become
As old as one another!

PICKUP TRUCK?

My brother's very proud today
He bought a pickup truck.
It's jumpy and it sputters, so
I call it hiccup truck.

EAT A CAR

I think I'd like to eat a car
   Just to say I could.
First I'd eat the doors and trunk
   Then I'd eat the hood.

I think I'd like the motor best-
   Pistons, points and plugs.
I'd gobble up the engine block,
   The tires, wheels and lugs.

Then I'd go inside the car
   To look for a dessert.
I'd finish off the dash and seats,
   Then I think I'd burp!

What kind of car is best to eat
   Convertible, van or coup?
Which would be the best one for
   Automobile soup?

I asked my dad to use his car
   To have myself a munch,
But he replied, "I'm sorry, Son,
   I ate my car for lunch!"

SLEEP

Barking dogs, croaking frogs
My brother's smelly feet.
I know that I am going to die
If I don't get some sleep!

SILLY SISTER

"Brush your hands
And wash your teeth
Before you go to bed.
Blow your clothes
And fold your nose,"
My silly sister said.

LIFE IS EASY

Life is pretty easy now
   As far as I can see,
Everything I need today
   Is being done for me.

The dishwasher is washing
   All the dirty dinner dishes.
Mother's at the supermarket
   Buying what's delicious.

Busy people in the streets
   Are everywhere around,
Building things, moving things
   And fixing up the town.

The libraries are taking care
   Of books I need to read.
People everywhere I look
   Are doing things I need.

The only thing I know of that
   Will cast a cloud of doom,
Is the fact that no one comes
   To straighten up my room!

THE RACE

I ran a race at school today,
  They said I came in last,
I didn't lose 'cause I was slow
  Because I ran too fast.

I know I was in perfect shape
  I had a lot of power,
I blew out both my running shoes
  At 90 miles an hour!

PURPLE PEOPLE

I knew a purple lady who
 Bought a purple couch.
She kept her purple husband in
 A velvet purple pouch.

The happy purple couple did
 A lively purple dance
For all their purple friends in
 Their printed purple pants.

Then all the purple people did
 The proper purple thing
They made a purple circle and
 Began to purple sing.

The pretty purple lady dropped
 Her spouse's purple pouch
On the wooden purple floor and
 He screamed purple ouch!

This funny purple story is
 About to purple end.
Have a proper purple day from
 Your wacky purple friend!

BIG KITE

My brother made the biggest kite
A beauty - like no other,
The wind came down and flew it up -
Uh Oh, where's my brother?

WIND

I felt the wind
Caress my skin
And blow my
Bushy hair.
It was so strong
It wasn't long
Before I wasn't
There!

MOODS

My moods are changing all the time
  Like channels on TV,
Depending on the one you choose
  You'll find a different me.

Here's my private channel guide
  To find the mood I'm in.
Pick the one you want today
  From one to number ten:

    Turn to channel one
    I'm ready for some fun,
    Turn to channel two
    I can play with you,
    Turn to channel three
    Stay away from me,
    Turn to channel four
    I'll be a little sore,
    Turn to channel five
    I'm feeling so alive,
    Turn to channel six
    I'm feeling kinda sick,
    Turn to channel seven
    I've moved it to eleven,
    Turn to channel eight
    I'm running kind of late,
    Turn to channel nine
    I'm feeling pretty fine,
    Turn to channel ten
    It's time for this to end-
    Turn it to eleven
    It takes you back to seven.

CAJUN ZOO

There are no animals at the zoo
  Down in Cajun land.
They cooked 'em all up in a stew,
  Except the few that ran.

27

MY NAME

Francois Dubois
T-Boy Lafitte,
Lassaire Monet
Pierre Petite,
 Bonin Chauvin
  Richard Rousseaux
  Monsieur Gaudin
  Louie Comeaux.

Now you know
My nickname . . .
My real name is
Beaux Beaux.

SCENE TWO: SCHOOL AID

Go to school
Follow rules
Take a lot of tests
Go to school
Follow rules
Try to do your best

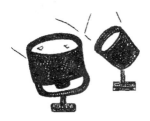

OLD SCHOOL RULES

There is a rule at every school
  A very basic principle,
You can make some big mistakes
  But never cross the principal.

Obey the teachers all the time
  No running in the halls,
Keep it quiet and never riot
  No writing on the walls.

Eat your food, don't complain
  And never ask for more,
Do not take another's cake or
  You'll be shown the door.

Raise your hand before you talk
  Remember what you learn,
No dogs or frogs allowed in class
  No speaking out of turn.

The rules sometime slip my mind,
  Too many to remember.
I will obey the rules today
  'Cause I'm a great pretender.

SCHOOL
RULES
1. NO DOGS OR FROGS
2. No ___ THE HALLS
3. EA___ ___OOD
4. DO___ ___IN
5. N___
6. ___

NEW SCHOOL RULES

Your homework isn't due until
   You've had a chance to play.
Teachers speak when spoken to
   And only then to say,

"Science class on the beach
   And English at the zoo,
A picnic for Arithmetic
   If you can count to two.

Social Studies will be held
   On cloudy rainy days,
The only grades that are allowed
   From now on will be A's.

For classes in Geography
   You have to catch a plane
To go on down to Kingston Town
   Then off to lunch in Spain.

The School Board and the Principal
   Must always be behaved,
'Cause if they break a single rule
   Their heads will all be shaved!"

SEA SCHOOL

I wish the waves
   Could be the teacher
And the beaches
   Were the classes,

I would make
   The Honor Roll
By counting
   Ocean splashes.

THE BIG TEST

This homework is too difficult
  I really have to struggle,
I think it takes a Wizard's brain
  And I am just a Muggle.

I'm feeling kind of sick today
  I cannot miss my class,
Tomorrow is the big exam,
  The one I need to pass.

I'm feeling low, my fever's high
  My head is getting hotter,
I could not pass that test today
  If I was Harry Potter!

MY GRADES

I got an A at school today and
   That's as good as it can B
But I am happy most of all
   When I get love, you C.

Now mom is sad and dad is mad
   When I bring home a D
And every time I bring one home
   It's awful: woe is me.

If you want to hear a noise that
   Surely makes you deaf
Just hang around to hear the sound
   If I bring home an F!

A CRIME

The world is not a perfect place
They tell me all the time.
How come when I flunked a test
They said it was a crime?

CATCH A TEACHER

Eeeney-Meany-Miney-Mo
Catch a teacher by the toe.
If she hollers, run away
Or it's you who's gonna pay.

WHAT I LEARNED IN SCHOOL TODAY

Next time that

My uncle says
My mother says
My father says
My brother says
My grampa says
My granny says
My neighbor says
My auntie says:

"What did you learn in school today?"
This is what I am going to say:

Dogs don't fly, flies don't bite and
   Cows don't swing from trees.
Snails don't jump, bugs don't sing,
   Cats don't dance with fleas.

Frogs don't cry, bears don't cook,
   Birds don't fly a plane.
Bees don't sneeze, fish don't fry and
   Snakes won't call your name.

As you can see, I studied hard and
   Gained a lot of knowledge
I cannot wait till I grow up so
   I can go to college!

SPACE KIDS

I'm going to go to outer space
  To check up on the moon.
You can go, just show up here
  We lift off right at noon.

Don't forget to tell your mom
  The trip will take a year.
Tell her not to worry much
  'Cause I know how to steer.

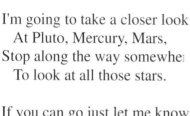

I'm going to take a closer look
  At Pluto, Mercury, Mars,
Stop along the way somewhe
  To look at all those stars.

If you can go just let me know
  It really will be fun!
I just remembered . . .
  I can't go -

    My homework
    isn't done!

I LOVE

Homework is my greatest joy -
  I love it more than food
I have to have some everyday
  To keep my pleasant mood.

I love the mathematics best
  And English I adore!
Examinations are a thrill
  And recess is a bore!

I've written to my Congressman
  To cancel summer break.
Ninety days without a class
  Is more than I can take!

My longest day is Saturday,
  And Sunday I'm depressed.
No classroom time on either day -
  I won't be getting dressed.

Will you join my homework club?
  We'll have a lot of fun.
I welcome all new members
  'Cause I'm still the only one.

NO SCHOOL FOR ME TODAY

Morning's here. It's 5 AM
I wonder how awake I am.

My arm is moving - not my knee
Am I awake? Not all of me.

I'll keep my legs right here in bed
The rest of me can go ahead.

The only problem with that is
Today in math we have a quiz.

If I went to school today
Without my legs I know they'd say:

Forgot your legs
You silly fool?
That's against
A rule of school.

You have to have
Your legs and feet
Or you don't get
To take your seat!

Do you really
Understand
You will miss
The math exam?

I might as well just stay in bed
After all is done and said,

I'll miss that math test anyway -
So I'm not going to school today!

SPELLING

I'm not too good at spelling words
That always make me stumble
Like pseudonym and homonym
Or words I have to mumble.

I like to spell the simple words
Like hee or shee or thay.
I do not like to spell such words as
Crawfish ëetouffee.

TRAVEL

Places that I hear about and
  Study in geography
Are places someday I will want
  To travel to and see:

Kilimanjaro
  Katmandu
    Costa Rica
      Mt. Maru
        Himalayas
          Amsterdam
            Mongolia
              Uzbekistan
                Tanzania
                  Zambia
                Chili and
                Colombia
              Venezuela
            Antilles
              Dominica
                West Indies
                Argentina
                  Mexico
                  Ecuador
                  And Tokyo
                Paraguay
              Bolivia
            Pakistan
          And India
       New Zealand
        Indonesia
          Malaysia
            Polynesia.

                (Wouldn't it be easier
                  to live in Polynesia?)

                A lot of
              Travel for today
              Let's go back
              To USA!

THAT
SPECIAL
POEM

Whoever you are
Wherever you are
A poem is waiting for you.

To find that poem
You need to read
A poetry book or two.

Skip the ones
You don't enjoy
And read until you find

That funny one
That precious one
That jumps into your mind.

The fairest one
And rarest one,
A simple work of art-

The poet knows
That one goes
Directly to your heart.

A LITTLE POEM

**I wrote a little poem today
It didn't have a lot to say.**

HOW TO WRITE A POEM

It's hard to write a poem they say,
It doesn't have to be that way,
Because when you just sit and stare
Sometimes it comes from pure
Thin air!

45

TWENTY-SIX LETTERS

With twenty-six letters
  In the alphabet
Look at the billions of
  Books that you get.

Twenty-six letters
  Are all that there are,
So many books
  They stack up to Mars.

Twenty-six letters are
  All that we've got
That's all that we have,
  Like it or not.

Twenty-six letters and
  All of those books,
Written by painters and
  Teachers and cooks.

Actors and poets and
  Novelists too,
There is probably one that
  Is written by you.

If twenty-six letters are
  All that are right
Will people run out of words
  They can write?

```
OXOXOXOX      XOXOXOX
OXOXOXOXOX    OXOX XOXOX
OXOXOXOXOXO   XOXOXOXOXO
```

A LOVING oxox POEM

When you're feeling kind of sad
And don't know what to do,
Find someone you
Care about and
Tell them,
I love
You.

A BIGGER POEM

This one is a
BIGGER poem,
taking center
stage.
It must be a
greedy poem,
it wants to hog
the page!

A POEM
FOR MYSELF

I bought some books of poems today
   To give myself a chance to play,
 I flipped and thumbed from line to line
   To find a poem with clever rhyme.

I looked and looked from book to
   Book but never could I find,
A single poem that pleased me more
   Than any poem of mine.

WHEN TO WRITE A POEM

When I am sad
I write a poem
To help me
Through the day.

When I am glad
I write a poem
To help me
Stay that way.

A FORBIDDEN POEM

This is a forbidden poem
   You're not supposed to see.
If you peek your eyes fall out,
   But don't come blaming me.

All I did was write this poem
   And warn you not to look,
I hope that you will never find
   This poem in any book.

So why are you still reading it?
   Now have you lost your mind?
What is it that makes you read
   This banned forbidden rhyme?

If you insist on reading more
   I feel compelled to say,
"Tonight while you are fast asleep
Your hair will fall away!"

SCENE THREE:
TUMMY TEASERS

Tummy teasers
Belly pleasers
Food you can adore
Tummy teasers
Belly pleasers
Food that is a bore.

CHARLIE AND THE OREO COOKIE

Oreo cookies are
Running down the street
Chasin' after Charlie Man
Looking for a treat.

Charlie Man, Charlie Man
Run, run, run,
Oreo cookies coming
One by one.

Cookie wanna Charlie Man
Charlie Man, Charlie Man
Cookie wanna Charlie Man
Gotta have one!

Oreo cookies are
Running down the street
Chasin' after Charlie Man
Looking for a treat.

Charlie Man, Charlie man
Run, run, run,
Oreo cookies coming
One by one.

Cookie ate a Charlie Man
Charlie Man, Charlie Man
Cookie ate a Charlie Man,
Yum, Yum, Yum!

CHOCOLATE TEST

I got an A at lunch today and
   Passed the chocolate tests.
My teacher said I should be proud
   I did my chocolate best.

See if you can pass them too
   The tests are down below.
Impress the teacher and your friends
   With all the stuff you know:

Test # 1

A chocolate bunny is so funny
   When it's melted on your tummy
Chocolate kisses are delicious
   When you kisses and you misses.
Chocolate candy what a dandy
   In your pocket it is h- - -y

Test # 2

There ought to be a special rule
   For chocolate lunch at every s - - - - l
Chocolate milk in all the fountains
   Chocolate trees and chocolate mountains.

Test # 3

Chocolate isn't really bad,
   Chocolate isn't just a fad,
All the chocolate doctors say
   Eat your chocolate every d-y.

I hope you also got an A.

THE MYSTERIOUS CASE
OF THE
HOLE IN THE BOWL

There's a hole in the bowl
Of my breakfast food.
I better clean up
Before I get sued!
There's milk in my lap
And goo on my shoe,
Flakes on the floor
And blueberries too.
A shirt full of sugar
All sticky and sweet -
Whoever's the culprit
I'd sure like to meet.
Was it Lucy or Linda
Or Lacy or Liz,
Freddy or Frankie
Or Willie B. Whiz?
This hole in the bowl
Of my breakfast food
Has got me upset,
I'm coming unglued.
I'll get me a lawyer
To check out the case
And sue for a million -
This is a disgrace!

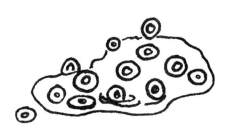

COOKIE CRUMBS

Cookie crumbs are all around
    In every room they can be found.
It's very hard to understand
    I've had no cookies in my hand.

It's not my fault, don't look at me.
    Look up there and you will see
The cookie jar is way up high,
    I think those crumbs have learned to fly.

INVITATION

The party starts at five o'clock
    And I'm inviting you.
I'll be cooking all the food and
    Trying something new.

Onion flavored oatmeal and some
    Slightly pickled pumpkin,
Sugar covered mushrooms with a
    Jell-O flavored dumpling.

Peanut butter, mashed potatoes,
    Rice and apple juice,
Scrambled eggs and gravy with a
    Mustard carrot mousse.

A pot of roasted skinny yellow
    Texas chicken feet.
There'll be lots of food around
    For everyone to eat.

If you haven't had enough when
   Everything is finished
We will have some extra fare like
   Sauerkraut and spinach.

If this is not your favorite food
   You don't need to worry
We are having mocha meat and
   Ice cream covered curry!

Saut'ed ketchup cookies cooked
   In cherry flavored bacon
Hot dogs boiled in honey and . . .

What?

Mom said I'm mistaken!

LUNCH KID

I've got jelly in my belly button
  Burgers in my nose,
Chocolate in my fingernails and
  Corn between my toes.

Chocolate mousse is in my hair
  Ice cream in my eyes,
Butter in between my fingers
  Chicken on my thighs.

Gummy bears are in my ear
  Potatoes in my skin,
A noodle wrapped around my head
  And drooping from my chin.

Every time I go to school
  I have a kind of hunch
That no one will invite me to
  Sit down with them at lunch.

DIET

Please don't make me drink my milk
   Or eat those blackeye peas
Don't make me eat zucchini cause
   It makes me cough and sneeze.

I cannot eat this broccoli or
   This cauliflower stew
I cannot swallow chicken and
   I'm not just kidding you.

I never ever want to see
   Another plate of liver
If I get too close to it, it's sure
   To make me shiver.

Don't serve me any poultry please
   Especially scrambled eggs
'Cause if I do then I will get
   A rash upon my legs

I have to strictly stay away from
   Eating bread and meat
I'll miss a lot of school because of
   Achy head and feet.

The other day I tried a plate
   Of southern rice and beans
It was a big mistake because
   It made me nice and mean.

The reason for this problem is,
   I'm from planet Mars
And the only foods that I can eat
   Are chocolate candy bars.

CAULIFLOWER

I've never read a single poem
  About the cauliflower,
How much people care for it
  How much they will devour.

I've never heard a singer sing
  A cauliflower song,
In the total scheme of things
  Where does it belong?

I've never heard of cauliflower
  Season celebration
Or seen it used by anyone
  As party decoration.

Could cauliflower be the most
  Neglected and abused-
Of all the healthy food we have
  Is it the most refused?

People say that cauliflower
  Makes you choke a lot
So when you eat your cauliflower
  Use some chocolat'!

HEALTHY LIVING

Eat your fruit and vegetables
  And only meat that's lean,
But drink a lot of water and
  Forget the coffee bean.

Vitamins will keep your body
  Working well and strong,
Getting sleep and exercise will
  Keep you living long.

Eating too much chocolate is
  A way of getting sick -
If you're asked to read a poem,
  This one you should pick.

Be sure to read this poem aloud
  Before you read the others,
Because this poem is written for
  Impressing all the mothers.

THE ICE CREAM STREAM

Deep in the woods
About 22 miles
Where few have ever seen

This stream, I'm told
Has no water
But runs with pure ice cream.

The ice cream stream
Never runs out,
With 28 different kinds:

Chocolate, cherry
Pink raspberry
And never has any lines.

You can walk right up
And help yourself
To a tasty sweet delight

'Cause there's enough
If the whole world came
Morning, noon, and night.

You needn't worry
If you fell in
It might be a little bit cool,

Down you would float
To where the stream pours out
Right into the pudding pool.

The only way out
Is to go underneath
The lollipop bubble gum gate

And if it's not open
And you can't pass
You just have to eat while you wait!

So, next time you go
Out to the woods,
Look for the ice cream stream.

You'll find the map
To where it is
When you go to sleep,
 and . . .
dream!

NUTRITION

If broccoli and spinach
Are better to eat than
Pizza, burgers and chicken to go,

Then why don't you see
Broccoli and spinach
Sponsor a vegetable television show?

A FRYING SAUCER

Gobbling Gourmet
  Giggling Nan
Fried in a saucer
  Instead of a pan.

Guzzling customers
  Gathered at noon
And voted her cooking
  The food of the moon!

DARKNESS IS FOR SLEEPING
BUT IT CAN BE USED
FOR SNEAKING

Late at night into the kitchen
Looking for the stuff,
That you were fed at dinnertime
But didn't get enough.

SMARTY JOE

I met a dog
  Named Smarty Joe,
Now he's a friend of mine.
  He's far too smart
To be for show
  He's got a brilliant mind.

"Oh well," said Joe
  One boring day,
"I think I'll read a book."
  He reached up to
The highest shelf
  For one called, "How to Cook."

"Oh, boy!" said Joe,
  "We'll have some fun
'Cause I will cook tonight."
  Now in the kitchen
He'd just begun
  When he saw a curious sight.

Through the window
  He put his head,
And said, "This looks weird to me!
  My master there
Sleeps in my bed
  While I cook dinner for three!"

GRACE

Bless this food
This festive mood
And all these loving souls,

Give us grace
And heightened taste
To empty all these bowls.

We are blessed
To have the best
Of all that we can measure,

But in the end
The gift of friends
Remains our greatest treasure.

SCENE FOUR:
ANIMALS,
BIRDS & BUGS

Cats and dogs and bugs and frogs
Are all my favorite friends
When I am home and all alone
I let them all come in!

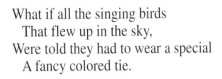

WHAT IF ANIMALS
HAD TO DRESS

What if all the singing birds
  That flew up in the sky,
Were told they had to wear a special
  A fancy colored tie.

And every single milking cow
  Put on their favorite shoes,
Before they got to walk around
  To say their morning moos.

Supposed they made a special rule
  That all the city cats,
Would have to go and buy themselves
  A blue designer hat.

And then they made the puppy dogs
  Wear sterling silver chains,
Before they got to play in any
  Puppy frisbee games.

What if all the croaking frogs
  Were spending all they had,
To fill the muddy froggie ponds
  With fancy lily pads.

Suppose the chickens wouldn't lay
  A single chicken egg,
Until they got to cover up their
  Skinny chicken legs.

What if fish that swim the seas
  And all the ocean whales,
Went to purchase Christmas stuff
  At Santa's clearance sale.

And all the different kinds of snakes
  Would not attempt to crawl,
Unless they got to wrap themselves
  In brightly colored shawls.

And wiggly worms refused to eat
  A single bit of dirt,
Before they got to button up their
  Favorite pleated shirts.

Suppose that all the honeybees
  Would charge a little money,
Before they give the beekeepers
  A single drop of honey.

This could make the world become
  A little more confusing,
But it could make a boring day
  A whole lot more amusing!

CATS AND DOGS

When you call a puppy dog
   He jumps into your lap.
When you call a kitty cat she
   Stays right where she's at.

FIDO

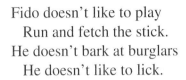

Fido doesn't like to play
  Run and fetch the stick.
He doesn't bark at burglars
  He doesn't like to lick.

Fido doesn't like to play
  With any kind of dog,
And he'd never chase a cat
  Because . . .

Fido is a frog!

DAPPER FROG

I know a quite capricious frog
  I think he's pretty weird,
He's got a hat, a walking cane,
  A moustache and a beard.

A graceful, handsome, dapper frog
  So suave and debonair,
He thinks it strange that other frogs
  Are bald and have no hair!

CITY DOGS

I wouldn't want to be the one
   To walk a dog in town.
When he poops you have to scoop it
   Right up off the ground.

Now you've got a stinky bag
   That's full of doggie doo.
I wonder if the doggie thinks that
   Baggie belongs to you.

DOGGIE THOUGHTS

I'd like to take a walk today
 I need a human being
Spring is bringing flowers out
 The bushes need a peeing.

Someone grab this leash for me
 And take me to the park
I've been behaving all day long
 It's time to walk and bark.

Let's go down to Cherry Street
 To Collie Clara's yard
I'd like to mark her fence again
 And give her my regards.

Stay away from alleys, please
 With all those scrubby dogs;
And whoever takes me out today
 I hope that you don't jog!

MR. O'TOOLE

We bought a new cat named Mr. O'Toole
  The minute we got him he started to drool.
He's spitting and drooling and dribbling so much
  His hair is too slimy and sticky to touch.

I awakened one night from a slumbering sleep
  To a slobbering, dribbling cat on my feet.
He dribbled and slobbered and tickled my ear
  For a week and a half I barely could hear.

When O'Toole is awake he's contented to sit
  And gobble and guzzle and dribble and spit.
He's never been able to corner a rat
  His body gets stuck wherever he spat.

Our family conducted a meeting today
  To decide if O'Toole was to go or to stay.
In spite of the dribbling and slobbering and such
  We decided to keep him, we love him so much.

MY ONLY PET

I used to have a lot of pets:

(A crocodile, a beetle bug,
a mockingbird, a garden slug
a rattle snake, a kitty cat,
a little furry guinea rat).

And now I have but one.

The beetle ate the slug, the
Mockingbird the beetle,
The rattlesnake, the mockingbird
And kitty cat, the guinea rat.

The crocodile was lying low
Relaxing in his nest,
At dinnertime he came around
And ate up all the rest!

TURTLE NAMES

We have to find another name
 For Susie's newest turtle
She has already eight of them and
And everyone is Myrtle.

How 'bout something that's unique
Like Yasalitta La Monique or
Dubie Billy Bobby Dan
Suey Su Wa Na No Nan

Or Laura Limpton Lanny Lu
La La Lisa, Lana Sue.
And if it sang the name could be
Music notes like Do Re Mi.

I think I know just what to do
If Susie doesn't mind,
We'll name the newest turtle
Mr. Turtle # 9.

THE MONKEY AND THE DONKEY

A monkey and a donkey were
  The very best of friends,
The monkey was the brother and
  The donkey was the twin.

Everything the monkey did
  The donkey tried to do,
The monkey went to climb a tree
  The donkey did it too.

The monkey and the donkey were
  Together everywhere
The donkey saw the monkey do and
  Picked the monkey's hair.

The monkey and the donkey wrote
  A monkey-donkey tune
They played it with a fiddle and
  They sang it to the moon.

The monkey showed the donkey how
  To do the monkey dance
The donkey danced the monkey in
  His dance-a-monkey pants.

The jolly happy monkey and
  His dance-a-monkey friend
Met up with a horsie and her
  Little rabbit twin.

The rabbit and the horsie from
  The horsie-rabbit land,
Danced the horsie-rabbit to the
  Rabbit horsie band.

The rabbit and the horsie and the
  Monkey-donkey gang,
Sat around the monkey house
  Until the monkey sang.

The monkey and the donkey and
  The horsie-rabbit team,
Did the funky monkey dance in my
  Monkey donkey dream.

PETS

Polar bears are
Cold and wet
I wouldn't have
One for a pet,
It would sleep
Inside the freezer
Mother said that
Wouldn't please her,
Panda bears are
Cute and funny
They do cost
A lot of money,
Got a bullfrog
For a joke but
I would die
If it would croak!

WOODPECKER PET

A man named Smith
   With a wooden leg
Was frightened to hear one day,

His nephew who owned
   A woodpecker pet
Was coming for the summer to stay.

HUMBLE BUMBLEBEE

Pardon me!

I accidentally
    Walked into a
Flying bumblebee.

He didn't even sting,
    Because he was
A humblebee.

PETER'S RABBIT

Peter was unhappy 'cause
His rabbit ran away.
Gloomy little Peter
Had
            A
          Bad
            Hare
              Day.

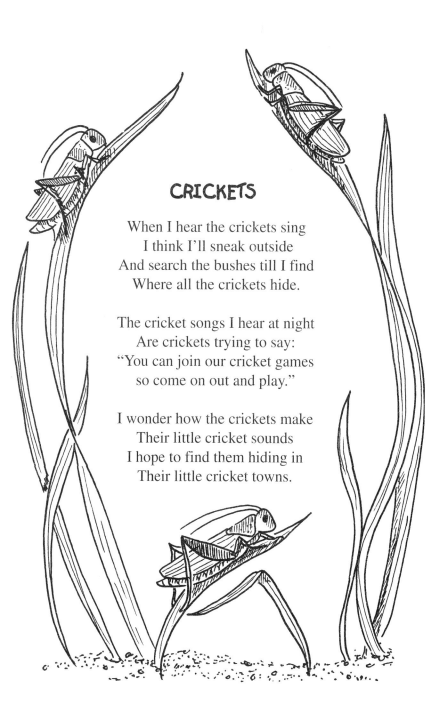

CRICKETS

When I hear the crickets sing
I think I'll sneak outside
And search the bushes till I find
Where all the crickets hide.

The cricket songs I hear at night
Are crickets trying to say:
"You can join our cricket games
so come on out and play."

I wonder how the crickets make
Their little cricket sounds
I hope to find them hiding in
Their little cricket towns.

ANTS

You don't see a lot of poems
 About the busy ant.
It's really not the poet's fault
 Not because they can't.

Ants can put the poet in
 A very sour mood
When they line up single file
 And eat up all his food.

VACATION

When snails go on vacation
   The never need to pack.
They don't make reservations,
   Their house is on their back.

FIREFLIES

On warm and muggy
   Summer nights,
Mosquitoes flashing
   Little lights,
Disappear
   When daylight ends
And come again
   When night begins.

MOSQUITOES

Mosquitoes out in Idaho
  Are really quite polite
They fly around and buzz your ear
  Before they land and bite.

Mosquitoes seen in New Orleans
  Are quite a different thing
They take your blood before you feel
  The slightest little sting.

If they like your kind of taste
  And want a little more
They can grow up big enough
  To open up the door.

Mosquitoes there are everywhere
  Looking for a snack
When they find a favorite kind
  They launch a full attack.

So now you know, in Idaho
  Mosquitoes there are nice,
But I have seen in New Orleans
  Mosquitoes big as mice!

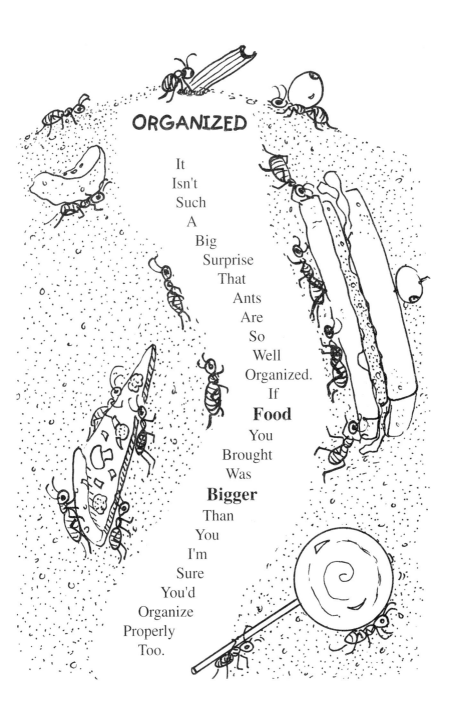

ORGANIZED

It
Isn't
Such
A
Big
Surprise
That
Ants
Are
So
Well
Organized.
If
Food
You
Brought
Was
Bigger
Than
You
I'm
Sure
You'd
Organize
Properly
Too.

THE FLY

The most persistent
  Thing on earth
Has got to be the fly.

The more you swat
  And swing at them
The harder they will try.

It seems as though
  They always know
The slap is sure to miss.

The fly is brave
  To risk his life
To steal a little kiss.

FLYING LESSONS

A bird can fly
From side to side
Around
And upside down.

When I try
To run and fly
I'm off,
Then on the ground!

BIG BIRDS

If birds were big as airplanes
    I think you would agree,
The world would be a very scary
    Dangerous place to be.

If birds were big as airplanes
    I think it could be said,
It wouldn't be too smart to have them
    Landing on your head.

If birds were big as airplanes
    I wouldn't want to be
Standing underneath a flock
    While flying over me!

SCENE FIVE:
PLAYING OUTSIDE

Night and day,
Rain or Shine
The place I want to be,
Is out of doors
Where I can find
Amazing things to see!

I LOVE TO BE OUTSIDE

I love to go and play outside
   No matter rain or shine,
With all the flowers, birds, bugs
   And furry friends of mine.

I love to watch a bunny hop
   And all the timid squirrels,
That come around to say hello
   Then vanish to their worlds.

I love to find a muddy lake
   Or ditch, or pond or stream,
Then lie beneath the open sky
   And take a nap and dream.

I love to be outside and see
   The evening catch the day
And watch it slowly disappear
   And softly slip away.

I love to look up in the night
   Into the starry skies
And watch the stars look back at me
   Into my starry eyes.

Soon it's time to go inside
   That's all for me today.
I'll sleep until the sun comes up
   Then go outside and play!

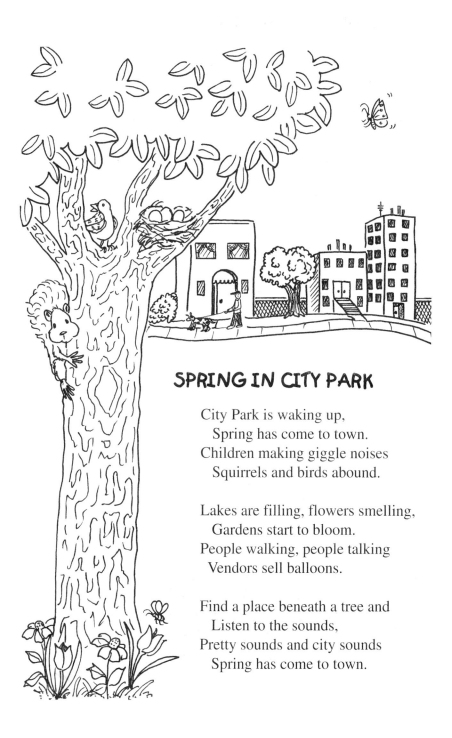

SPRING IN CITY PARK

City Park is waking up,
  Spring has come to town.
Children making giggle noises
  Squirrels and birds abound.

Lakes are filling, flowers smelling,
  Gardens start to bloom.
People walking, people talking
  Vendors sell balloons.

Find a place beneath a tree and
  Listen to the sounds,
Pretty sounds and city sounds
  Spring has come to town.

SUMMER FLOWERS

I see the meadows blooming with
   Mountain summer flowers,
I'm standing in the middle of the
   Rainbow summer showers.

I feel the sun upon my face,
   Hidden joy rekindles
Summer warmth embraces me,
   Winter sorrow dwindles.

Summertime has given me these
   Meadows full of reasons
To celebrate this fascinating
   Mountain flower season.

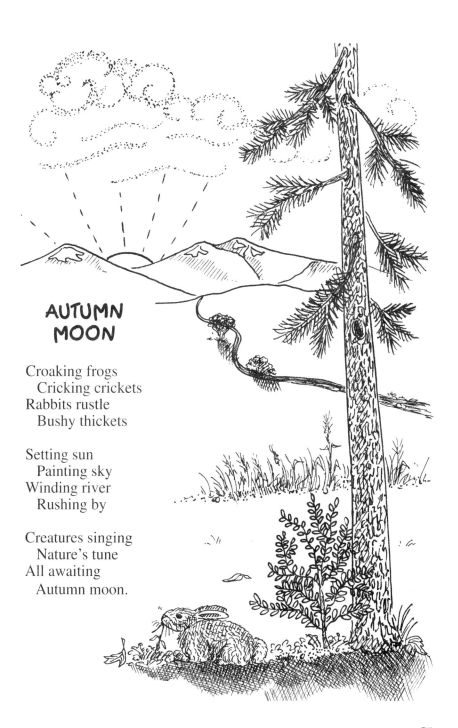

AUTUMN MOON

Croaking frogs
  Cricking crickets
Rabbits rustle
  Bushy thickets

Setting sun
  Painting sky
Winding river
  Rushing by

Creatures singing
  Nature's tune
All awaiting
  Autumn moon.

MY SPECIAL FRIEND

I have a very special friend whose
Name I do not know
I never heard him say a word,
    All he does is grow.

He is a very faithful friend and
    Always comforts me,
He seems to really understand,
    My friend, the Willow Tree.

STARS

I wonder if the stars at night
So high up in the sky,
Are looking down at us on earth
Into our starry eyes.

SOLITARY MOON

I saw up in the sky tonight
A solitary moon
It looked just like it came out of
A fantasy cartoon.

I gazed up at the moonlit sky
Into the outer space
It's hazy, yellow, golden light
Was coloring my face.

I think that I will write a song
That has a catchy tune
And sing it by the lighting of
The solitary moon.

TWILIGHT

The end of day
  Is soft and sweet
It's summertime in June
  Orange and yellow
Painted sky
  Making way for moon.

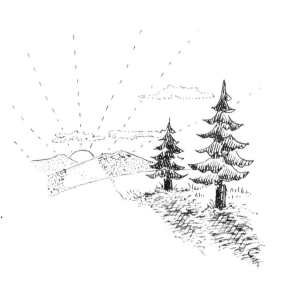

HORIZON

There's a place where the sky
  And the ocean meet,
A place I've never been.
  Maybe that's where heaven is
And forever will begin.

THE PICNIC

The picnic starts at two o'clock
   I'm bringing all my stuff,
Umbrella, raincoat, boots and hat
   I hope I've got enough.

The weather turned out beautiful
   No reason to complain,
The sun was shining bright and clear,
   But I was dressed for rain!

THUNDER

If I could fly like eagles fly
I'd soar right up to a cloud,
And look in there
At all that air
To see what makes the thunder loud.

RAIN

Falling from the sky above
   Clouds begin to sneeze
I'm taking cover underneath
   Weeping willow trees.

Rain has started pouring down
   Drips turn into drops,
Cuddled up beneath the trees
   I wait until it stops.

GARDENING

Flowers that my mother plants
   Never make me sneeze
Flowers that my brother plants
   Always make me wheeze.

My mother loves her garden
   It's the place she likes to be,
She has a garden angel there
   To keep her company.

KEEPING WARM

Whenever I'm cold
  And want to get warm
I just go put on a sweater.

When animals are cold
  They know how to grow
Their fur for the wintry weather.

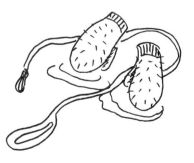

GRATITUDE

It's time to go inside for now
And slip into a dream
And say a prayer of gratitude
For all that I have seen.

SCENE SIX:
PONDERING

Pondering and wondering
Thinking all the time-
Pondering and wondering
Secret thoughts of mine

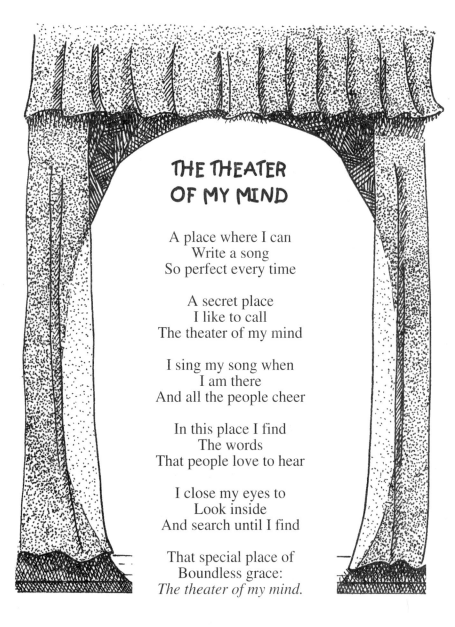

THE THEATER
OF MY MIND

A place where I can
Write a song
So perfect every time

A secret place
I like to call
The theater of my mind

I sing my song when
I am there
And all the people cheer

In this place I find
The words
That people love to hear

I close my eyes to
Look inside
And search until I find

That special place of
Boundless grace:
The theater of my mind.

MY FAVORITE DAY

My favorite day is Saturday
  A sit with you and chatter day.
Sunday is a funny day
  A joking and a laughing day.

My worst day is a Monday
  A getting back to school day,
And Tuesday is a choosing day
  A picking you and me day.

Wednesday is a friendly day
  A be with all of you day,
Thursday is a wordy day
  A reading and a writing day.

And Friday is a my day
  And a do what I can do day,
I think I'll make a new day
  And I'll call it I love you day.

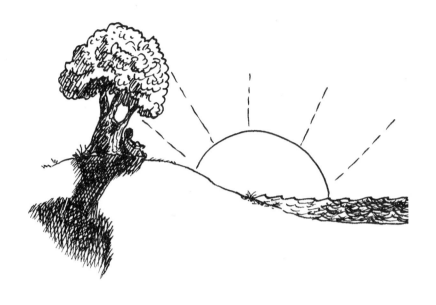

TODAY

Yesterday
Has gone away
Today
Is all I've got.
Tomorrow
Will become today
And yesterday will not.

POINT OF VIEW

The cheerful boy to the playful dog:

"A beautiful warm
and sunny day,
no rain has come
to spoil our play."

The frightened fish to the worried frog:

"A miserable dry
and thirsty day,
no rain has come
to fill our bay."

BIRD IN THE HAND

A bird in the hand
Is worth two in the bush
Never made sense to the bird.

Nature requires
At least two in a bush
In order to create a third.

A bird in the hand
Will eventually die,
Nobody's prayers or wishes

Will ever restore
That beautiful bird to
Sing again in the bushes.

I'D RATHER BE ME

I'd rather be something I am than
   Pretend I am something I'm not.
Do everything I possibly can
   To keep whatever I've got.

I'll always know that whenever I go
   And wherever I happen to be
The person that I am able to show
   Is the authentic original me.

GROWING UP

I never want to grow,
I told my mom and dad
I'd miss the me I know,
And that would make me sad.

DREAMERS

I'm a dreamer
You're a dreamer
They are dreamers, too.

When evening
Comes we fall asleep
And do what dreamers do.

I WONDER

Could a tree grow taller
  If there wasn't any sky
Or a reason be an answer
  If it didn't have a why?

Could day become dawn
  If there wasn't any night
Or the night become dark
  If there wasn't any light?

Could the feelings of love
  Then really be there
If there wasn't any you
  Or a someone to share?

Could there ever be a yes
  If there never was a no,
Would there ever be a kid
  If he never got to grow?

Could there ever be a world
  Like the one that we can see
If there never was a you
  Or there never was a me?

ME

If I could be
Whatever I see
What I would be is a me.

A me is a me
And I am a he
And never could I be a she.

When I was three
She said to me;
"I'm glad that I'm not a he.

So she and me
As you can see
Are happy that we are a we.

TREE HOUSE

Ann and Jill
And Bob and Me
Built a house up in a tree.
We tried to pick a proper name
But none of us would pick the same.
Bob said *he* house, Ann said *she* house.
Jill said *we* house, I said *me* house. So Ann
And Jill and Bob and me talked and we could not
Agree. He wouldn't call it *she* house. She wouldn't
Call it *he* house. I wouldn't call it *we* house, we wouldn't
Call it *me* house. So Ann and Jill and Bob and me talked until
We did agree and now we call it
Tree
House

YOU

I've taken a liking
To someone
Striking,
Who's personable,
Pleasant,
Gracefully elegant,
Delightful,
Pretty,
Charming and witty.
Can you guess
Who?
That's right, it's
You!

LAW OF LOVE

Whenever I give
  I get more love,
A definite dependable fact.
  Whenever I do
Open my heart,
  Love comes doubling back.

A HAPPY THOUGHT

When I have a happy thought
  I save it in my mind,
In case I need to use it for
  Another sadder time.

GLAD TO SEE YOU

My tummy tickles
  Deep inside
When I hear you say

That you are glad to
  See me and
You'd like for me to stay.

My heart is happy
  When you take
My hand and smile at me.

When you are here
  There's no place else
On earth I'd rather be.

ADVICE

Here's what children
Need to know . . .
Keep on laughing
As you grow!

About the Author
Frank Lloyd Kramer

Frank has recently appeared on the national scene as a popular poet. His first book, *Cats, Dogs, Bugs and Frogs*, was produced in 1995 and has sold out. Since then Frank has written hundreds of new poems which he has been sharing with elementary school kids who have encouraged him to publish this book. He's also written five other books: *Tales of Tails from Snails to Whales, What If Animals Had To Dress, Poems About Poems, The Cajun Poet*, and *Playing Outside: Rain or Shine*, which he hopes to have published soon. Frank's poetry has appeared widely in numerous children's magazines and the educational market. Frank was born in a small town on the banks of the Bayou Teche, in South Louisiana. He now lives in Denver, Colorado with his wife, Lynn Sauve who is contributing editor and designer. His grown daughter also lives in Denver.

About the Illustrator
Vickie Leigh Krudwig

Vickie is the author of the Award-winning book, *Cucumber Soup* (Fulcrum Publishing Company), *Hiking Through Colorado History* (Westcliffe Publishers), *Christian Bulletin Boards* (Instructional Fair, a division of T.S. Dennison), *Wings Upon the Water - A Fisherman's Legacy*, Illustrator for *Taming the Tornado Tube* (by Steve Spangler), Illustrator for *Cats, Dogs, Bugs and Frogs* (by Frank Lloyd Kramer). Vickie has also written articles for *Highlights Magazine*, *Wild Outdoor World*, and *Kid City Magazine*, Vickie lives in Denver, Colorado with her husband and three children.